STOP WOR

GW01390798

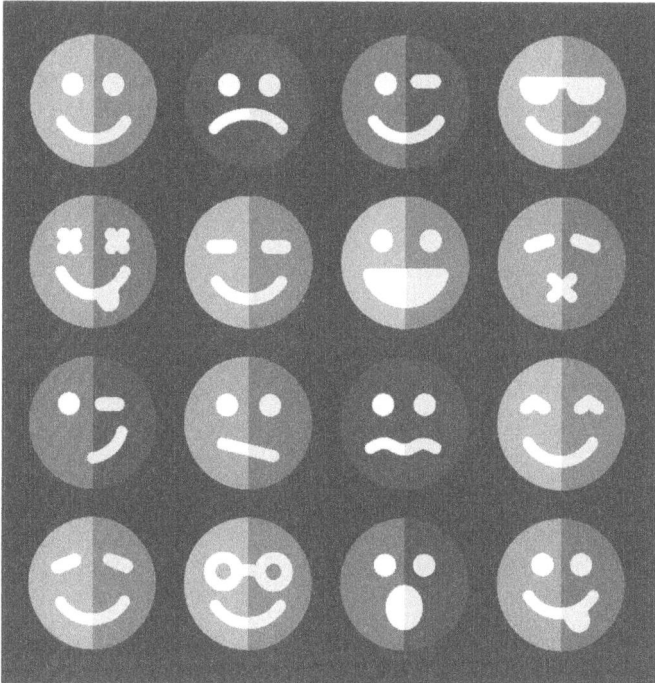

Rid yourself of worry and release

your anxieties

i

STOP WORRY NOW

Rid yourself of worry and release
your anxieties

Feel good

Achieve your potential in life

by

Whingers Tannah

Printed and bound in Great Britain by CompletelyNovel.com

First Printing, 2015

ISBN: 9781849148306

For the real you!

CONTENTS

INTRODUCTION

It's all about today, here and now, because for that moment in time what else is there? But how did you get to today? And where do you go from here? These two questions are continuously polling through our minds whether we like it or not. It can be very easy for us to become preoccupied with our own history and futures to the extent that it can take over our lives and manifest itself into a permanent state of worry and anxiety.

For Myself, I used to be what is commonly referred to as a born worrier although you wouldn't know it to look at me or speak with me, because I'm also a very good actor, skilled in the art of concealing the real me. I'm now glad to say that all of this has now changed and I have now learned how to start living my life in a more rewarding manner. Through the medium of this book I will show you how to do the same.

I remember how I used to say to myself why do I feel like this? And what is that whirring feeling inside my stomach? Thinking that I've got to get away from here. So what is this all about and why did it only seem to affect me? And was it only me who felt like this?

Of course it wasn't a continuous feeling, there were many moments where it didn't trouble me at all, but I found it impossible to pinpoint when it would hit me hardest which didn't make it easy to address.

So how and why did it start? To be truthful nobody could possibly know. There are all kinds of possible theories, all of which I have self-evaluated. These would range from a high dependence on my parents due to a childhood illness, overprotection as a result, getting in with the wrong group of friends at school, 'dodgy' girlfriends, tyrant bosses, etc., etc., etc. Basically, this was everybody else's fault except mine. But whatever the cause it doesn't matter anymore. It dawned on me that it's time to move on and to stop wasting any more time thinking about the causes. Easy for me to say, I bet you are thinking, but just trust me with this for the time being - there is no need to continue apportioning blame for your worry and anxiety. It had taken me years to get to this point, so please force yourself to believe me and all will become clear!

My development over the years had been very gradual to the point where I eventually had that lightbulb moment. From that point onwards my life started to change. But don't get me wrong, even before then, I refused to allow worry and the anxiety born from worry to take over my life completely. I still had a good time, was lucky enough to meet my wife and have three terrific children, whilst also forging a good career in I.T. But the worry was always there and was holding me back from being my real self and achieving what I really wanted from life.

Now, if there was a self-help article or book available on the subject, then I would read it. Whilst these helped me to expand my mind to new ideas and approaches to life, they did not help me address my problem. So what was I worried about?

We are all driven by ambition, whether this refers to career or personal goals, there is drive within us all to succeed. I have always been ambitious professionally and I think that to a certain extent some anxiety has helped me along the way, acting diligently and conscientiously in all I did, but that might be me just putting a positive spin on it! Overall, continuous worry causes tension which triggers anxiety - a perfect recipe for a downward spiral into despair.

So what changed? The simple answer is ME! Or more precisely my mind. The techniques I used to overcome my worry and years of anxiety were alarmingly simple to implement to the point where I was amazed that it took me so long to work it out. But as they say sometimes it's hard to see the wood for the trees.

So, who am I and what makes me think that I am qualified to help you? Well, by day I am an IT Professional, with over twenty years of experience working within both large global organisations as well as smaller consultancies. Along the way I have mentored and trained a number of friends and colleagues throughout their careers. By night, as they say (and if I'm truthful by day) I was a worrier, troubled by anxieties born out of over thinking.

So, as a result I have done my fair share of research into worry and how we operate and as I am sure there are many people who are experiencing what I have, then maybe what I can share will also help them.

When writing this book, I was mindful of how I used to feel, I needed something that was concise and quick to implement, which is hopefully what I have provided for you here.

So without further ado, please read this book as many times as you feel necessary and rid yourself of the worry curse that plagues many of our lives.

Enjoy and start living!

1. WORRY AND ITS COMPONENTS

It doesn't matter who you are or what your age or social standing is; there is a simple truth and that is that we all worry. It is impossible not to. But whilst some worry helps us to stay safe and motivate us into action, excessive worry can limit us and sometimes destroy lives.

So how can we define worry? Our minds are incredibly powerful and complex with the ability to process tens of thousands of thoughts every single day. Despite this, we are only capable of thinking about one thing at a time, surprisingly we are not able to process multiple thought patterns simultaneously. So how does this help us to understand worry? Well, I will do my best to explain.

Our brains react to circumstances that appear to present real physical danger triggering what is called the 'fight or flight' response. This response is designed to keep us safe and at the time of a threat our thoughts are dominated by this reaction. Over time, we have evolved significantly as human beings creating 'relatively' safe environments in which to live in comparison to our ancestors. Unfortunately, parts of our brains have not evolved at quite the same rate, therefore, we find it difficult to sometimes add perspective to situations – more on this later.

The worry of immediate threats to our wellbeing is only a small part of the story. Our minds do not operate on idle very well and are continuously hunting for something to occupy them. To try and explain this further, think of your thoughts in three categories:

The **PAST**

The **PRESENT**

The **FUTURE**

The **PAST** is your history. Your achievements to date, relationships to date and everything that life has thrown at you. You can do nothing to alter anything that has already happened up until THIS very moment in time. Sounds obvious doesn't it? But this is crucial in understanding part of the worrying process.

Have you ever heard the expression 'stop living in the past'? Well that is exactly what a number of us are doing on a regular basis. Do you ever feel really low after returning home from vacation? Or when you say goodbye to friends or family after they visit you? Well, this is a perfectly normal reaction, however, some people struggle to deal with these emotions and unless the mind is 'distracted' these feelings can develop into worry leading to anxiety and then sometimes to a state of depression. The vacation example might sound obvious, after all, most of us don't like returning to everyday life after a holiday, but let's try to understand our feelings and how we deal with them. Many of us work hard all year long to save enough money for some form of a break from the cut and thrust of everyday life. So what occurs in your mind when your holiday ends and you return home? If you are anything like me then you will probably be longing for that beach you left behind or saying phrases to yourself like 'this time last week I was by the pool in my hotel', be honest we have all done it. But once again this is normal behaviour, and then all of a sudden memories fade a little and the monotony of everyday life takes over and this brings your mind back into the 'present'. This example is based on recent 'historical' events that impact your emotional state of mind and it could be argued that it is not so much worry that we experience here, more a case of sadness or feeling depressed.

Let's be clear here, one of the reasons worry affects us in the way that it does is that our thoughts often take us back to historical events, whether pleasant or not so pleasant, the effects on our physical wellbeing are the same. Pleasant events create a feeling of longing; 'what if I never experience this again'? Or 'why can't it be like it used to be'? Non-pleasant events create feelings of trepidation, whether consciously or sub consciously you fear for a reoccurrence of such circumstances. Bizarrely, we worry about all of these events that have already happened, concerned and fearful that these pre-determine what is going to happen next in our lives.

The **PRESENT** is all around us. Just take a brief moment to stop reading and look up. You are in the process of creating history this very minute, okay, it might not be life changing history, but nether-the-less it is still history. If we are genuinely consumed by the present moment, then we are not concerning ourselves with what has already happened or what might happen in our lives in the future. When we worry about our immediate circumstances we don't have time to dwell on or contemplate them to the extent that our emotions become depressed. Instead we are more focused on dealing with the issue in front of us, so the 'fight or flight' reaction will be triggered. The 'fight or flight' response creates a number of physical sensations within us, such as an increased heart rate, excessive sweating, diarrhea, to name a few. The approach for dealing with short term threats or worries differs to that for historical triggers as you will discover later within this book.

Unfortunately, our brains process non-physical and physical threats in the same way, so the danger associated with an imminent physical attack (such as a wild animal) will have a similar immediate impact on us when we receive tasks that are outside of our comfort zone, such as the demand to deliver a presentation.

Finally, there is the **FUTURE**. Dominated by the 'what ifs' and the 'what is going to become of me' scenarios that we as human beings like to continually question. For many of us, it is very hard not to predetermine our futures in our minds by what we already know about the past. For instance, we all have dreams, but how many of us really believe we can turn these dreams into a reality? The answer is not many of us, because we are restricted by what we perceive to be our limitations.

So how do we worry about the future? Well, the answer is very complex and I am not going to pretend to you that I fully understand it. However, to deal with the worry associated with the future, we only need to be able to appreciate from a high level the associations involved. When we start worrying about the future our thoughts are also connected to the past. An example of this would be delivering a presentation in front of a large audience. Now for those that are accomplished at giving presentations and have been in such circumstances on numerous occasions before, the worry levels or fear would be lower than for those who are relatively new to the experience. This is because the mind, either consciously or sub-consciously will recall previous similar situations. For those with more experience, there are likely to be successes, therefore, convincing the mind they are capable of succeeding again. This in turns allows the individual's thoughts to focus more on the content and delivery style of the presentation, rather than the actual task of giving the presentation itself.

Another example to illustrate the past to future connection would be how we react to a relationship ending. So you have been with someone for a significant period of your life and then one day it is over! Whether you saw it coming or not, it can be just as hard to deal with, so how does your mind want to react? Maybe with a feeling of regret, relief or even denial, this obviously depends on the circumstances surrounding the split, but more often than not, your immediate thoughts start to think about the future and this is where the worry is born. Where do you go from here? Can I fix this? Will I ever find anyone else or happiness? What if I end up all alone? So you can see why we might start to worry in such circumstances.

All of this may sound very depressing in itself, but hopefully it provides a brief insight as to how our minds can operate when it comes to worry. The good news is, we are going to learn how to deal with the worry later within this book.

2. HOW WORRY

MANIFESTS ITSELF

When we worry, our bodies and emotions react and change accordingly. If there is something pre-occupying your mind, such as a change in your life or a forth coming event, your 'regular' life may feel like it has been placed on temporary hold as you struggle to focus on anything else. If you are 'lucky' enough to have a very busy life then ironically this can be an advantage when dealing with such dominant thoughts and your mind becomes distracted from dwelling on what has been worrying you. Unfortunately, such respites can be few and far between, because your mind will want to focus back onto those worries as soon as it becomes idle again. Remember that your mind can only process one thought at a time, so if you are worrying about something this must be dominating your thinking patterns, unless worry has just become habit, which is also possible.

Your body also reacts to these thought patterns. As part of the 'fight or flight' response we've already mentioned such reactions as increased heart rate and sweating, but there are other non-obvious impacts such as the effect on appetite and the ability to digest food efficiently, a feeling of nausea along with overall fatigue can be common.

When we start to recognise these reactions to worry, it is then easy to become caught up in the cycle of worry, where you are not only worrying about a specific change or event, but also worrying about the worry itself. Eventually, if this cycle is allowed to continue, our health starts to deteriorate and the world becomes a dark and gloomy place in which to live.

3. THE LIMITING

EFFECTS OF WORRY

Worry can trap us within our own lives and stop us from achieving what we are really capable of, undermining our very existence. Short term worry, whilst being a normal human response, will only have a limited effect on our lives; whereas prolonged periods of worry can lead to anxiety and significantly undermine our personalities and confidence. Confidence in ourselves is the key to our happiness and is the major influencing factor to our successes and achievements in life.

So how is worry linked to confidence? If we are worrying about something that we have control over, such as giving a presentation or performing well at a particular sport, then this worry is born out of fear, fear of failure which is likely to be linked to the perception we have of ourselves when placed in such circumstances. Our confidence can be eroded away by previous 'disasters', negative feedback or persistent worry where we always consider the worst case scenarios. If we cannot control our worries for such occasions then we cannot possibly hope to perform at our best. Our confidence thrives when we are successful, so however small the success, it is important to bank these achievements and start to grow and develop as individuals. But we also need to be able to accept failure in such a way that our confidence and belief systems remain intact and protected.

4. THE SLIPPERY SLOPE INTO LIFE'S ABYSS

So what can happen to us if we do not deal with our worries? Suppose we were to let our worries (no matter how big or small) dictate how we live our everyday lives. Well, to a certain extent we are all guilty of allowing them to do so. Do we still function? Yes, but our effectiveness, happiness and ambition may not be at a level to make any difference to anything that we would want to achieve.

Many of us go through life wondering 'what if' or 'if only' rather than grabbing life by the 'scruff of the neck' and making things happen. We all know that life is hard, there are very few people who can go through life without a care in the world, but what we occasionally see is an individual who radiates happiness or confidence and we start to assume that they are the lucky ones who have fallen on their feet. To some people, happiness is nothing more than being happy – a state of mind, regardless of what trials and tribulations are going on behind the scenes of their lives. Try it! Whatever the circumstances are, try smiling and humming a tune for ten minutes and feel your mood lift. To most of us though it is hard to focus beyond our worries and the impact can be devastating.

I am going to make an assumption that you are reading this book because you are troubled by worry and are looking for solutions. So, with that in mind, stop thinking about what you are reading and instead I want you to think about your face and your shoulders. Is your face screwed up or tense? Are your shoulders slightly raised? If you are honest with yourself, you will probably agree that they are, and I bet you didn't even notice it before you started thinking about it.

The impact of worry and anxiety is not only physical, it goes much deeper than that, into the dark reaches of your subconscious mind. As previously mentioned, worry is linked to confidence and if you haven't even the desire born from confidence and determination to get up and tackle the world each morning, then what is left? You owe it to yourself and your very existence to deal with your current circumstances and associated worries so that you can start living the life you deserve. It is now time to stop wishing your worries away, hoping for life to deal you a good hand, because it won't and you will spend the rest of your days feeling hard done by.

I am not going to allow myself to become too morbid about where people can end up if they allow circumstances and worry to dictate their lives, but I believe that there are three stages before reaching the abyss of despair:

- Worry
- Anxiety / Stress born from worry
- Depression

As I have already mentioned, we all worry, but we do not all allow worry to lead onto the subsequent stages above and it is my intension to make sure that you don't either. All of this is easy to say, but how do we go about coping with worry? In the following chapters I cover a technique for dealing with both 'past and future' associated worries along with a coping mechanism for addressing immediate worry situations. All you need to do now is read on, understand and practice them for yourself.

5. TECHNIQUE TO STOP WORRYING

Visualise a triangle, with equal length sides.

Place yourself within the triangle and mentally label the sides, Past, Present and Future.

Position yourself (mentally) so that you are facing the side labelled Present, the other 2 sides (Past and Future) should only be visible in the periphery of your vision.

Now in your mind, focus only on the side labelled present, consciously blocking the other 2 sides from being allowed into your mind.

Now you are ready to begin and with practice you will automatically be able to recall this mental image with ease when required.

To begin, wherever you are and whatever you are doing, place yourself in the present, right now, only visualising the present moment – use the triangle imagery above to shut off the past and the future. For this moment in time it doesn't matter what has gone before or what it going to happen in the future.

Pay real attention to your surroundings, mentally record what you can see, look at the colours and materials in front of you, take it all in.

Use as many of your senses as possible to appreciate the present moment.

THEN STOP!

Go back and focus on your worries, notice that I didn't say stop worrying and never will, as that doesn't work. If you are not entirely sure exactly what is worrying you, it may be lots of things, then stay in the present moment.

Finally, focus again on the present moment – appreciate it for what it is, but this time consciously think about your next immediate course of action that will occupy the next hour or so of your life. Whatever it is, however mundane it might be, commit yourself wholeheartedly to making this next hour of your life an absolute joy and success. So, even if it is just popping to the shops to pick up some provisions, enjoy the experience, force yourself to smile, maybe hum a tune, speak to and acknowledge as many people as possible, treat yourself to a chocolate bar or something that you wouldn't normally buy, you get the idea.

If you really commit yourself to the experience you will be amazed as to how good you start to feel. All of a sudden you will start to release some of the burdens that have been weighing you down and you may even feel exhausted when you get home, but you will also feel rewarded. Now after a little more practice, try doing the same for multiple periods throughout your day and then for consecutive periods, so joining 2 hours together at a time. After a few weeks of effort doing this, something remarkable will start to happen. Your new committed approach to life will start to become a habit and a natural way of operating. You will soon find that your days are more fulfilled and the time spent worrying is significantly reduced.

This technique will help you to achieve more out of your day, however, it will not stop you from worrying altogether, nothing can do that. As soon as your mind becomes idle again, there is every chance new worries will be triggered or it may bring up older ones, but now you have a mechanism of moving these to one side whilst you get on with your life.

Initially this will require practice, so look at doing this at least 3 or 4 times per week and if possible even on multiple occasions on the same day.

If you commit to this and really believe it will work (which it will) then brace yourself to welcome the new more positive you.

6. DEALING WITH WORRYING SITUATIONS

Every so often in our lives, we are put on the spot or something totally unexpected is presented to us, triggering bouts of worry and anxiety. How can we cope in such circumstances so that our performance is not significantly impaired?

Here is a method for dealing with worry and anxiety on the spot:

1. Look at the problem and immediately start to analyse it, don't park it away to the back of your mind – it will keep nagging away.
2. Break it down if applicable into manageable chunks.

3. Determine what the very worst outcome could be?
4. Process the worst case scenario and start to accept this as a reality.
5. Look at the options available to improve upon the worst case scenario.

Our minds are strange oddities in that when they start to accept the inevitable, however bad, they start to move into a more relaxed state enabling us to start dealing with the issue at hand. All of a sudden things do not seem that bad after all. Give it a try, what have you got to lose?

7. SET GOALS TO GET MOTIVATED

So with some practice and real application it will not be very long before you start to feel that you are taking control of your worries and anxieties. In addition to this it is very likely that your new positive approach to life will open new doors, bringing new opportunities and relationships along the way. But where do you want to take your life from here? What is it that you would really like to achieve and why?

The next step is to start setting some goals for yourself, both short and long term ones. These goals must be achievable and realistic and where possible linked, to be used as stepping stones for achieving something 'big'.

Whatever your ambition or overall goal is, it is important when starting this process to make them as small as possible, whilst still remaining purposeful. As you start to achieve your initial goals and targets, continue to set new, more challenging ones, whilst all the time remaining focused on the 'bigger' picture if possible and the ultimate goal you wish to achieve.

Throughout the process, it is fair to say that there will be both good and bad days. It can be difficult to continue ploughing through tasks working towards goals on a daily basis, so DON'T. Make sure that you give yourself a break and some time off, occasionally revisit the technique and coping mechanism for dealing with worry, stay on top of things.

When you start to re-immerse yourself into achieving new goals, have a bigger picture and overall goal clear in your mind. It is this bigger picture which will keep you going and fire up your motivation. When motivation starts to wane, STOP, take time out and re-assess your goals and progress to date, making sure that you are on the correct path.

IDENTIFY GOALS AND

TRACK THEM

1. Identify short term individual goals and record progress.
2. Set 3 or 4 'bigger' goals that you would like to achieve.
3. Map your route for achieving these goals, breaking them down into smaller sub-goals.
4. Record progress as you go against each goal, not matter how large.

NOTES

Lightning Source UK Ltd.
Milton Keynes UK
UKOW06f1555120716

278226UK00001B/44/P

9 781849 148306